# THE BIOGRAPHY OF TOBY KEITH

## THE LIFE AND LEGACY OF A MUSIC ICON

**JAMES STEVE**

*THE BIOGRAPHY OF TOBY KEITH*

# COPYRIGHT BY THE AUTHOR
# ALL RIGHT RESERVED

# Table Of Content

# Chapter 1: Background and Early Life

One of the most recognizable characters in country music, Toby Keith, has a life narrative that embodies the spirit and essence of American music. He was born in Clinton, Oklahoma, on July 8, 1961, and grew up in a household that enjoyed storytelling and music. From a small-town kid to a multi-platinum recording artist, Keith's path is replete with inspirations, obstacles, and pivotal events that molded his creative style.

## 1.1 Early Life and Family Factors

Keith was surrounded by the rich American Southwest culture while growing up in Oklahoma. Hubert Keith Covel, Toby's father, was a significant influence in his early life and was a member of the US Army. His mother, Joan, was a housewife who instilled in her kids a passion for music. The Covel home was always filled with music, and Toby was influenced by a variety of genres from an early age.

Keith was raised by his mother and sister after his parents divorced when he was a little child. His mother's passion for music persisted throughout the family's turmoil. Toby's own songwriting was eventually influenced by the narrative and melodic styles of legendary country musicians like Johnny Cash, Merle Haggard, and George Jones, whom Joan introduced to him.

Toby has always had a natural talent for music. He developed his theatrical talents by taking part in school plays and local talent events. When he started to play the guitar as a teenager, his interest in music grew. He was introduced to a wide range of musical genres by the Oklahoman local scene, but he was especially attracted to the storyline of country music since it connected with his background and life experiences.

Singing and storytelling were common during family get-togethers, which emphasized the value of customs and legacy. Toby's passion for narrative-driven songs was developed by these events, which would eventually show itself in his songwriting. The basis for the issues Keith would portray in his music, especially the virtues of family, hard work, and perseverance, was placed by his childhood, which was both difficult and joyful.

## 1.2 Starting Out in Music

When Toby Keith was a teenager, he really started his musical career. He began doing stand-up in local Oklahoman pubs and clubs at the age of fifteen, where he could show off his skills and interact with the public. In addition to helping him hone his skill, these early concerts gave him an idea of what a music career may entail.

Following graduation, Keith tried a number of careers and kept up his side gigging as a musician. As a roughneck on oil rigs, he gained personal knowledge of the labor-intensive way of life that would subsequently inspire his music. Keith joined the band "Easy Money," where he played lead vocals, since he was determined to be successful in the music industry. They performed at local establishments and honky tonks, gradually gaining a local following.

Keith relocated to Tucson, Arizona in 1982, where he carried on with his performances and career development. He also started writing his own songs around this period, incorporating his own experiences into the lyrics. Genuine and approachable, Keith's work often drew inspiration from the setbacks and victories of daily life. His perseverance in perfecting his skill ultimately paid off when he attracted the interest of insiders in the music business.

Keith's self-titled first album, which included the smash song "Should've Been a Cowboy," was published in 1993. Being one of the most played country songs of the decade, the song shot to the top of the charts quite quickly. Toby Keith's early breakthrough brought him into the public eye, but it also signaled the start of a difficult road in the music business, one filled with setbacks and rejections.

## 1.3 The Early Years and Challenges

Keith had difficulties in his early career despite his early success. Keith had difficulties negotiating the intricacies of the music business, which is known for being unpredictable. Following the economic success of his initial album, his following releases did not do as well, raising questions about his standing in the business. But instead of giving up, Keith was motivated to improve his sound and creative direction.

Midway through the 1990s, Keith was faced with a decision. He made the decision to remain loyal to his origins by putting classic country components into his work, while many other singers were embracing the pop-infused sounds of country music. Although it was a bold choice, it eventually defined his career and set him apart from many of his peers.

He also started to write and produce a greater percentage of his songs during this period, taking on a more prominent position in his music. With this change, he was able to express his identity as an artist and exercise more creative authority. This transition was evident in his 1996 album "Blue Moon," which appealed to listeners with a blend of modern country and honky-tonk sounds.

Keith had to deal with personal issues in addition to his music, including the demands of celebrity and how it affected his family life. It was difficult for Keith to juggle his growing career with his paternal obligations, but he never wavered in his dedication to his family or his music. His experiences as a husband and parent served as inspiration for many of his songs, which strengthened his bond with his listeners.

Toby Keith's dedication started to pay off by the late 1990s. His breakthrough single, "How Do You Like Me Now?!" from his 1999 album "How Do You Like Me Now?" cemented his place in the annals of country music. The album received several honors and recognitions in addition to being a commercial success. Fans of Keith's music were drawn to his narrative quality and honest lyrics, which often mirrored the ideals and realities of working-class Americans.

Keith's early years were crucial in molding him as an artist. They were marked by family influences, musical discovery, and the difficulties of navigating the music business. Resilience, diligence, and genuineness values that he was taught as a child became pillars of his music and public character. Toby Keith stayed true to his beginnings as he rose to prominence in the country music industry, putting his experiences into songs that would come to define his career and resonate with millions of listeners.

The early years and upbringing of Toby Keith serve as a testimony to the narrative and connection-making potential of music. His early life experiences, musical upbringing, and early professional setbacks prepared the way for a fruitful career spanning many decades. Keith left a legacy that appeals to admirers of all ages by staying loyal to the principles that molded him even as an artist. This basis prepared the audience for the influential music and cultural contributions he would make throughout the course of his career.

As a result of his early struggles and victories, Toby Keith became a voice for millions, capturing the experiences, principles, and resiliency of the American people. His tale shows how a person's life experiences can influence their art and establish a strong connection with fans, which has made him one of the most iconic characters in the history of country music.

# Chapter2: Ascent to Notoriety

The story of Toby Keith's ascent to prominence is one of skill, tenacity, and a strong connection with his heritage. Keith's career has been molded by important turning points, chart-topping successes, and partnerships. From his humble origins in Oklahoma to his current status as one of the most well-known figures in country music, his path is noteworthy. This chapter explores the critical events that thrust him into the public eye, starting with his breakthrough hit "Should've Been a Cowboy" and on through his later albums and partnerships.

## 2.1 "Should've Been a Cowboy": A Breakthrough

Toby Keith's self-titled first album, which included the hit song "Should've Been a Cowboy," was released in 1993. After peaking at No. 1 on the Billboard Hot Country Songs list and staying there for an incredible five weeks, this song became a cultural sensation. Its popularity was more than simply a business success; listeners connected with it because of its sentimental themes and narrative approach, which brought back memories of Keith's beloved traditional country origins.

"Should've Been a Cowboy" is the embodiment of the classic country story, which is a lament over missed chances and a desire for a more straightforward and daring existence. A large audience responded well to the song's appealing melody and realistic lyrics, which made Keith a new face in the country music industry. Keith's career would be marked by recurring themes of desire for the freedom and adventure associated with cowboy culture, as embodied in the chorus, "I should've been a cowboy, I should've learned to rope and ride."

Due to the song's popularity, Keith shot to national prominence and received praise and respect. It became one of the 1990s' most popular country hits and is now a mainstay of Keith's live appearances. "Should've Been a Cowboy" had an influence that went beyond the charts; it made Toby Keith a prominent figure in the country music scene and paved the way for his subsequent pursuits.

After making this discovery, Keith's momentum kept growing. He started building a unique reputation as a country artist as soon as he realized how important it was to take use of his newfound status. His genuineness and dedication to classic country themes made him stand out in a music scene that was moving more and more in the direction of pop-infused sounds. His commitment to sharing true tales and experiences gained him a devoted following of admirers who saw his sincerity as a defining characteristic of his work.

## 2.2 Important Hits and Albums

Toby Keith recorded a number more albums after the success of his first album, which helped to further establish his reputation in the country music industry. The smash track

"Who's That Man," from his 1994 second album "Boomtown," peaked at number one on the country charts. The album, which combined classic country sounds with modern elements, demonstrated Keith's development as a composer and singer.

"Blue Moon" (1996), one of Keith's most important albums, signaled a turning point in his professional life. The CD demonstrated his flexibility as an artist with a blend of upbeat songs and love ballads. "I Want to Talk About Me," the lead single, shot to No. 1 on the charts and became a huge smash, solidifying Keith's status as a hitmaker. His ability to engage listeners with sympathetic subjects and appealing songs was shown on this album.

Keith's album "How Do You Like Me Now?!" was published in 1999, and it would go on to define his career. The album's title track, which chronicled Keith's career in the music business, was an anthem of tenacity and self-assertion. Anyone who has encountered hardship may relate to the song's message of resistance and persistence. The song's huge commercial success saw it rise to the top of both the country and pop charts, greatly increasing Keith's fan base.

With the publication of "Pull My Chain" in 2001, which included successes like "I Love This Bar" and "Courtesy of the Red, White, and Blue (The Angry American)," Keith's ability to write accessible anthems continued. The latter became a national anthem for the United States, especially after the September 11 attacks. Many Americans were moved by the song's poignant words and picture of the armed forces, and Keith's unapologetic patriotism was well received by his fans. With this song, Keith cemented his reputation as a cultural analyst and country music artist by utilizing his platform to promote patriotism and military devotion.

Keith issued a number of more successful albums in the 2000s, such as "Shock'n Y'All" (2003), which included the popular track "American Soldier." His reputation as a patriotic musician was further cemented with this song, which pays homage to the American troops' sacrifices. Keith gained a devoted following by connecting with a wide range of people via the skillful blending of personal stories with larger themes of perseverance and patriotism.

He became well-known in the country music industry thanks to his steady string of successes that reached the top of the charts and his many accolades, which included several Academy of Country Music Awards and Country Music Association Awards. Keith was a beloved musician who touched many Americans emotionally with his music, which delighted listeners of all ages.

## 2.3 Partnerships and Effects

As Toby Keith's career developed, he started working with other musicians and producers, which expanded his catalog of songs. These partnerships greatly influenced his sound and increased his exposure in the music business. During the late 1990s and early 2000s, Keith worked with producer James Stroud to create his characteristic sound, which is one noteworthy partnership. Keith was able to remain loyal to his country origins while pursuing new artistic opportunities because of Stroud's influence.

Keith worked with people outside of the studio. He promoted a spirit of friendship within the country music genre by regularly sharing the stage with other musicians. He collaborated with Alan Jackson on the song "I Don't Need Your Rockin' Chair" in 2003. It was a lighthearted duet that emphasized their mutual respect as musicians while showcasing their divergent talents. Keith's ability to combine his voice with others while retaining his own style made the song a fan favorite.

Keith's career was further aided by his partnerships with composers like Scotty Emerick. Emerick co-wrote many of Keith's songs, including "I Love This Bar" and "Beer for My Horses," which he co-wrote with Willie Nelson and went on to become another big smash. This song demonstrated Keith's narrative skill and capacity to relate to listeners on accessible issues. It was a lighter perspective on drinking and friendship.

Other genres' influences were also very important in forming Keith's musical approach. He often blended pop and rock influences into his country songs to appeal to a larger audience. Songs like "Get Drunk and Be Somebody," which has a more lively, rock-infused sound while retaining the narrative quality of country music, demonstrate his ability to merge genres.

Keith has influenced not only certain musicians but also the country music industry as a whole. He was motivated to become a composer by the narrative skills of renowned people like George Jones, Johnny Cash, and Merle Haggard, whom he grew up idolizing. Keith drew inspiration from these legends for his music, which is characterized by themes of perseverance, hard effort, and genuineness.

Keith has also been a steadfast supporter of the country music industry throughout his career, often voicing his opinions on the significance of upholding classic country traditions while welcoming innovation. Because of his dedication to the genre, he is well-liked by both fans and colleagues.

Keith's versatility as an artist is shown by his inspirations and partnerships. His capacity to interact with a wide range of artists and take inspiration from other genres has helped him to develop while being true to himself. As his career developed, he established himself as a major player in the country music industry by being recognized for his contributions to the industry in addition to his chart-topping successes.

The tale of Toby Keith's ascent to prominence is one of tenacity, genuineness, and a strong connection with his roots. Keith's career in the music business is a testament to his constant dedication to approachable themes and storytelling, starting with his breakthrough song "Should've Been a Cowboy" and continuing with the release of important albums and collaborations that helped form his style. His long legacy as one of country music's most cherished musicians has been cemented by his ability to write anthems that speak to a wide range of listeners.

Keith's legacy is still strongly rooted in the principles of perseverance, hard effort, and a love of music even as he continues to grow and inspire new generations of artists. Toby Keith's journey has not only won over fans' hearts but also permanently altered the country music scene, guaranteeing that his voice will be heard for years to come.

# Chapter 3: Genre and Style of Music

Toby Keith is often seen as a link between classic country music and modern sounds, personifying the genre's development throughout time. In addition to pushing boundaries and venturing into uncharted musical areas, his work exhibits a profound awareness of the origins of country music. This chapter will define country music, explore Keith's influence on modern country music, and evaluate his distinctive sound and lyrics.

## 3.1 Country Music's Definition

The folk music traditions of the southern United States are largely responsible for the early 20th century emergence of country music. It is distinguished by the use of uncomplicated melodies, simple harmonies, and often moving narration. Over the years, the genre has changed dramatically, inspired by a variety of musical genres like rock & roll, jazz, and blues. Fundamentally, a large audience can relate to country music because it often touches on themes like love, adversity, rural life, and the human experience.

Understanding country music's cultural origins is crucial to understanding it. Known as "honky-tonk," traditional country music is deeply rooted in the lives and experiences of working-class people. In the 1920s and 1930s, musicians like Jimmie Rodgers and the Carter Family were among the trailblazers who laid the groundwork for the genre, stressing narrative-driven lyrics and straightforward instrumentation, such as banjos, fiddles, and acoustic guitars.

Artists like Hank Williams, Johnny Cash, and Merle Haggard brought a more refined sound to country music as it developed throughout the middle of the 20th century, all the while upholding the narrative legacy. As the genre developed further, it gave rise to subgenres as pop country, outlaw country, and country rock, each of which brought fresh perspectives and inspirations.

Country music has been fusing with other genres more and more in recent years, giving birth to a new subgenre called "bro-country," which is defined by party themes and a more sophisticated production style. The authenticity of the genre has been a topic of discussion in the country music community as a result of this progression.

Nevertheless, narrative and emotional expression continue to be at the core of country music.

This diverse tapestry of inspirations and styles is captured in Toby Keith's songs. He has continuously incorporated modern elements into his music while staying true to his traditional country origins, making it listenable to both newcomers and die-hard country aficionados. His longevity in the country music industry may be attributed, in part, to his adeptness in navigating its always changing terrain.

## 3.2 Distinctive Melody and Poetry

Toby Keith's distinctive style, which blends elements of rock, pop, and even honky-tonk with conventional country instruments, is a trademark of his musicianship. Electric guitars, drums, and violin are often used extensively in his songs to produce a sound that is both modern and traditional. With this combination, he can create memorable tunes that appeal to a wide range of listeners while staying true to the roots of country music.

Another distinctive feature of Keith's music is his vocal delivery. His rich, rich voice carries a feeling of authority and genuineness that engrossed listeners in the stories he tells in his songs. Keith's delivery, whether it is an energetic song or a moving ballad, is distinguished by its emotional weight, which enables listeners to identify with the tales he shares.

Keith is well-known for his ability to narrate stories in poetry. His songs often touch on issues of love, family, nationalism, and the daily hardships faced by Americans in the working class. His ability to craft relevant storylines that mirror his listeners' lives is very evident. Songs like "I Love This Bar" honor the community that flourishes in local bars and the friendships that may be discovered there. Fans are emotionally moved by the song's lyrics, which vividly depict the lives and events that take place in these settings.

Conversely, Keith's overt patriotism and reaction to the events of September 11, 2001 are evident in songs like "Courtesy of the Red, White, and Blue (The Angry American)". His reputation as a spokesperson for American principles was further cemented by the song's combative tone and powerful imagery, which encapsulated the national attitude of the moment. Keith uses his poetry to connect with his audience's cultural and emotional landscapes in addition to providing entertainment.

Keith is not afraid to take on contentious subjects in his poetry, which is another noteworthy quality. He tackles themes of justice and revenge, for example, in songs like "Beer for My Horses," fusing comedy with seriousness in a manner that encourages listeners to consider larger social concerns. His ability to strike a mix between serious themes and lightheartedness distinguishes him from many other modern country musicians.

Furthermore, Keith often incorporates personal anecdotes into his songs, which lends credibility to his stories. His songs are appealing to a broad audience since they often depict the setbacks and victories of ordinary life. Keith establishes a connection with listeners by his sharing of personal anecdotes and insights that goes beyond the music itself.

## 3.3 Effect on Modern Country

The impact of Toby Keith on modern country music is substantial and varied. He was an artist who came to prominence in the 1990s, and at a period of significant transition in the genre, he was instrumental in determining its direction and sound. In addition to growing his fan base, his skill at fusing classic country characteristics with contemporary sensibilities has made it possible for other musicians to follow in his footsteps.

Keith's role in the marketing of country music is among his most significant contributions. A new generation of country musicians that aimed to cross genres and appeal to wider audiences was made possible by his success. Pop-infused country music has become more popular as a result of this trend, as seen by performers like Florida Georgia Line, Luke Bryan, and Carrie Underwood. These musicians often take cues from Keith's ability to craft songs that appeal to a diverse audience by fusing relevant words with appealing tunes.

In addition, Keith's unreserved acceptance of his cultural beliefs and patriotism has established a standard for other musicians in the genre. His songs resonate with listeners who respect music that matches their lives and ideals as they often praise the American identity. The music of performers like Jason Aldean and Brantley Gilbert, who have also adopted themes of perseverance and pride in their country, demonstrates this focus on patriotism.

Keith has had an influence on not only the genre of country music but also the business as a whole. He has been an outspoken supporter of artists' rights and has often spoken out against unjust business practices. There is a rising trend in the music business toward more artistic freedom as a result of his attempts to retain creative control over his work and motivate other artists to assume leadership roles in their professions.

In addition, Keith's dedication to honesty and storytelling has sparked a comeback of story-driven songs in modern country music. The narrative legacy is still a fundamental component of the genre, even with the increasing prevalence of pop elements. A new generation of songwriters who want to create comparable emotions in their listeners has been impacted by his ability to emotionally connect with listeners via sympathetic lyrics.

In addition, Keith's success in the digital era has shown the value of marketing and brand development in the music business. He has promoted his music and engaged with fans via social media and digital channels. This strategy, which emphasizes the value of audience involvement and connection, has set the standard for modern musicians navigating the rapidly evolving music business.

Country music has never been the same since Toby Keith's contributions and distinctive musical style. Keith has created a distinctive style that appeals to audiences of all ages by fusing classic components with modern influences. Fans are able to relate to him on a personal level because of his narrative skills and accessible songwriting, which enable them to recognize themselves mirrored in his songs.

Keith's influence may still be heard in the new and veteran musicians' work in country music as it develops. His dedication to storytelling-driven songwriting, patriotism, and sincerity acts as a beacon for the genre, guaranteeing that the fundamental principles of country music remain relevant despite shifting tastes in music. In addition to influencing the sound of modern country music, Toby Keith's skill has helped to strengthen the bond between performers and listeners, preserving the essence and vitality of the genre.

# Chapter 4: Ethics and the Individual Life

In addition to his music and notoriety, Toby Keith's life has been molded by his relationships, community involvement, and personal ideals. Keith has shown that his influence goes beyond the stage by focusing on family, charity, and activism throughout his career. This chapter examines Keith's political beliefs, family history, and charitable endeavors to show how these aspects of his life intersect with his identity as a person and an artist.

## 4.1 Relationships and Family

Hubert and Joan Covel welcomed Toby Keith into the world on July 8, 1961, in Clinton, Oklahoma. Keith was raised in a humble household and was taught the value of perseverance and hard work from a young age. His mother encouraged her children's passion for music, while his father a veteran of the U.S. Army worked many jobs to provide for the family. Keith had a strong respect for family values from these early familial experiences, which shaped his connections with others throughout the course of his life.

In 1984, Keith tied the knot with Tricia Lucus, his college love. Their relationship has been a pillar of his life, giving him security and encouragement throughout his turbulent ascent to stardom. Shelley, Krystal, and Toby Jr. are their three children together. Keith has spoken a lot about the value of family and how, in spite of the demands of his work, he makes time for the people he cares about. His ability to manage his career and family responsibilities is shown by the fact that he often takes his family on tour with him and involves them in a variety of initiatives.

As a parent, Keith has spoken freely that he wants his kids to grow up with strong morals. He has told them tales of his experiences instilling in them the value of diligence, decency, and fortitude. Keith often explores family and relationship issues in his songs, drawing on his own experiences as a husband and parent. For instance, he emphasizes the value of family ties and the values passed down from earlier generations in songs like "Daddy's Money."

Another source of inspiration for Keith's songs has been his marriage to Tricia. He has often shown his respect for her and acknowledged her as a stabilizing influence in his life. Fans have shown interest in their ongoing love story because they value the sincerity and dedication they embody. Many listeners find resonance in Keith's depictions of love and family in his songs, which serves to reinforce the values he finds important.

Keith has kept close ties with his friends and extended relatives in addition to his personal family. He often talks positively about his childhood in Oklahoma and the tight-knit neighborhood that molded him. Keith's ties to his former self serve as a constant reminder of his origins and the principles that still govern him.

## 4.2 Charity and Involvement in the Community

Giving back and helping those in need are two of Toby Keith's key principles, which are shown in his dedication to charity and community participation. He has participated in a great deal of philanthropic work during his career, concentrating on topics that are close to his heart and reflect his experiences and values.

The Toby Keith Foundation was one of Keith's most well-known charitable endeavors when it was founded in 2006. The goal of the foundation is to assist families and children who are undergoing cancer treatment. Keith has devoted a great deal of time and money to helping young cancer patients and their families find support, hope, and healing because he was inspired by their suffering. The foundation has contributed to a number of projects, such as the building of Oklahoma City's "OK Kids Korral," a cutting-edge facility that offers families and treatment-seeking children a cozy and secure space. Families may find a helping community at The Korral, which provides housing, food, and leisure activities during trying times.

Keith has raised millions of dollars for a variety of organizations via his foundation and participation in other concerts and charitable events. It is also striking how committed he is to helping veterans and active-duty military members. Keith's 2003 publication of the patriotic song "Courtesy of the Red, White, and Blue (The Angry American)" struck a chord with a lot of people, particularly those who were involved in the military. With the goal of helping soldiers adjust back to civilian life, he has actively sponsored groups like the **USO** and Wounded Warrior Project.

Keith does more for the community than just giving money; he often utilizes his position to advocate for causes that are dear to his heart. His involvement in programs that promote health care, education, and disaster assistance shows that he really cares about improving the lives of others. He often emphasizes the value of being involved in the community via his performances and exhorts his audience to do the same.

Keith's charitable endeavors are a reflection of his own ideals, which emphasize the value of kindness, community, and service. He has become a recognized figure in the philanthropic community as a result of his desire to help people in need and support causes that are dear to his heart, demonstrating that his impact goes beyond music.

## 4.3 Political Opinions and Campaigning

Over his career, Toby Keith's political activism and opinions have attracted a lot of attention. He has spoken his thoughts on a variety of subjects using his platform as an artist, often showcasing his dedication to American principles and patriotic beliefs. Keith is a strong supporter of veterans and active-duty military members, as seen by the themes of nationalism, patriotism, and support for the military that often appear in his songs.

Following the September 11 attacks, Keith became a well-known spokesperson for American patriotism. His song, "Courtesy of the Red, White, and Blue (The Angry American)," captured the determination and rage that many Americans were feeling at the time and went on to become an anthem for many. Audiences that felt the same way were struck by the song's powerful message of support for the armed forces and a plea for justice. Keith was positioned as a major voice for patriotic expression in country music as a result of this reaction.

Although Keith has a devoted following because of his patriotism, it has also caused controversy. Some have criticized him for his outspoken opinions on matters like as foreign policy, the military, and government acts. Keith has never been afraid to voice his ideas; he often discusses politics in interviews and in his songs. He has become a divisive figure in the country music industry due to his propensity to participate in political debate, which reflects the larger rift in American culture.

Keith has supported musicians' rights in the music business in addition to his patriotic causes. He has been a strong opponent of unethical business practices and a proponent of more openness and assistance for artists. His efforts to increase consciousness about issues impacting artists prove his dedication to enhancing the field for next cohorts.

Keith's personal values and political ideas are closely aligned, as he values upholding one's convictions and lending support to those who serve the nation. He has become a prominent figure in the country music industry as well as the larger cultural scene due to his ability to tackle contentious subjects via his songs and public remarks.

Toby Keith's identity as an artist and a person is fundamentally shaped by his personal experiences and principles. His dedication to activism, charity, and family is a reflection of his enduring faith in the value of genuineness, community, and service. Keith has shown by his connections and charity work that his influence goes beyond music, positively impacting many people's lives.

His family life emphasizes the virtues of love, support, and resiliency, which forms the basis of his values. Simultaneously, his charitable undertakings, especially via the Toby Keith Foundation, demonstrate his commitment to helping the underprivileged and giving back. Keith's political views and activism serve as more evidence of his dedication to speaking up for what he believes in and supporting worthy causes even in the face of criticism.

Toby Keith's personal life and ideals continue to be central to his identity even as he develops as an artist and a person. He has made a lasting impression on his fans and on the country music industry with his music, charitable endeavors, and activism. In the end, Keith's life narrative is one of sincerity, perseverance, and a strong desire to change the world, guaranteeing that his influence goes far beyond his artistic achievements.

# Chapter 5: Accomplishments and Acknowledgment

In addition to being one of the most successful musicians in country music history, Toby Keith is a notable individual whose achievements have had a considerable impact on the business. His transformation from a little-known musician to a household celebrity is shown by his many honors, achievements, and lasting legacy. This chapter looks at Keith's accomplishments, his effect on the country music scene, and his enduring cultural influence.

## 5.1 Honors and Submissions

Toby Keith's impressive career has been dotted with several accolades and nominations that attest to his creative achievements. Keith has had several Grammy nominations and over 20 chart-topping hits since making his breakthrough in the early 1990s. He has established himself as a major player in country music by winning important prizes from several organizations.

Among Keith's most illustrious achievements is his "Academy of Country Music Awards (ACM)" nomination. "Male Vocalist of the Year" in 1994 and "Entertainer of the Year" in 2003 are just two of the many ACM Awards he has received. His album "Shock'n Y'All" took home "Album of the Year" at the ACM Awards, solidifying his position as one of the industry's best. Keith has received several honors for his songs, which are well-known and have cultural importance, including "Should've Been a Cowboy" and "Courtesy of the Red, White, and Blue."

In addition, Keith has won " Country Music Association (CMA) Awards", including "Musical Event of the Year" for his song "Beer for My Horses" with Willie Nelson. He is well-liked in the business because of his capacity to establish strong bonds with other artists and produce remarkable partnerships. He has gained notoriety in a variety of musical circles for his work with different producers and musicians, which demonstrates his dedication to progress and cooperation.

Keith has received recognition from the "American Music Awards (AMA)" and the "Billboard Music Awards" in addition to his ACM and CMA honors. Numerous nominations for **Favorite Country Male Artist** have been extended to him, and his hits have often topped the Billboard charts. Keith's several gold and platinum certifications from the Recording Industry Association of America (RIAA), which recognize the album and single sales milestones, are proof of his commercial success.

In addition to conventional music honors, Keith has been acknowledged for his services to charitable causes. He received the **Spirit of Hope Award** from the **USO** in recognition of his dedication to helping American service members and their families. His charitable endeavors, especially those made possible by the Toby Keith Foundation, demonstrate his commitment to giving back and further solidify his standing as a versatile musician. All things considered, Keith's many accolades and nominations throughout the course of his career are a testament to both his skill and diligence as well as his capacity for building personal connections with audiences. Peers and fans alike have acknowledged his contributions to country music and his influence on the business, cementing his reputation as one of the genre's most renowned performers.

## 5.2 Impact on the Field of Country Music

The country music business has been greatly and diversely impacted by Toby Keith. He is a well-known artist in the genre who has influenced country music's style and sound for many years. He has been instrumental in the development of the genre, setting the path for a new generation of performers with his ability to fuse classic country components with modern sounds.

Keith's ability to communicate stories via his music is one of his greatest talents. His compositions connect with listeners on a human level since they often mirror feelings and events from real life. Other country music musicians have been inspired to use storytelling as a core component of their work by this emphasis on songs with a storyline. Keith's popularity with songs like "I Love This Bar" and "American Soldier" demonstrates how audience members can relate to and identify with personal issues, which can then become generational anthems.

Keith has also made a strong case for preserving the genuineness of country music. He has always stressed the value of being loyal to the genre's origins throughout his career and has often voiced his reservations about country music's growing commercialization. His dedication to traditional principles has encouraged many other musicians to put authenticity first in their work, preserving the core of country music.

Apart from his dedication to genuineness, Keith's acceptance of crossover components has shaped the style of modern country music. His use of pop, rock, and even hip-hop components into his compositions has allowed other musicians to experiment with a greater variety of musical influences. As a result of these genre blendings, subgenres have emerged, such as "bro-country," which is distinguished by its lively, party-focused themes and catchy songs. Keith's approach has served as an influence for musicians like Florida Georgia Line and Luke Bryan, illustrating the changing face of country music.

Beyond only his musical taste, Keith has influenced the industry's commercial practices. Many musicians have been motivated by his resolve to take charge of his career and make autonomous judgments about his music in order to defend their right to creative autonomy. Aspiring artists may use Keith's successful relationships with several record companies and his skillful self-promotion as a guide to help them navigate the intricacies of the music business.

Furthermore, Keith's support of veterans and active-duty military people has shaped the way that themes of patriotism and national pride are explored in country music. His songs have a strong emotional impact on listeners who have similar principles, strengthening the bond between country music and American identity. The emphasis on patriotism has inspired other artists to tackle similar subjects in their own works, strengthening the genre's ties to a sense of national identity.

All things considered, Toby Keith has had a significant impact on the country music scene. His devotion to authenticity, desire to try new musical things, and narrative prowess have had a lasting impression on the genre. His influence therefore keeps changing the course of country music and motivating a fresh round of musicians.

## 5.3 Cultural Impact and Legacy

Beyond his successful songs and several honors, Toby Keith's influence reaches deep into American culture and the ideals he upholds for both the country music industry and the broader public. His music appeals to listeners of all ages, solidifying his status as a revered personality in the music industry.

Keith's dedication to sincerity and genuineness in his lyrics is among the things that make him so iconic. His openness to discussing personal experiences and tackling real-life problems has helped him build strong bonds with listeners. Songs like "American Soldier" honor the sacrifices made by service members and their families, while "Should've Been a Cowboy" expresses the desire for a more straightforward and daring existence. Keith has amassed a devoted following of people who value his genuineness because of his relatability.

Keith has had a huge cultural impact on the country music industry. Many of his admirers have found solace in his unapologetic patriotism and appreciation of American principles, especially during times of national unrest. His music gave listeners a way to express their pride, rage, and sadness in the wake of 9/11, fostering a feeling of community. Following the tragedy, his song "Courtesy of the Red, White, and Blue" became an anthem for many Americans looking to show their patriotism.

Keith's charitable endeavors, in addition to his musical accomplishments, have solidified his reputation as a kind person who is committed to serving others. He has helped children with cancer and their families via the Toby Keith Foundation, making a significant and long-lasting difference in the lives of many people. His dedication to give back has encouraged other members of the business to take part in charitable endeavors, promoting a culture of giving and service within the country music industry.

Keith's influence on culture goes beyond his charitable work and musical contributions; it also includes his position as a public spokesperson for the liberties and rights of artists. His outspoken position on matters impacting musicians has sparked conversations within the field and created a feeling of camaraderie among musicians standing up for their rights. Keith has established himself as a recognized voice in the music industry by speaking up for what he believes in. His actions have an impact on how musicians manage their careers and deal with the financial side of music.

In the long run, Toby Keith's legacy will probably have an impact on next musicians and the development of country music. His ability to combine classic components with modern sounds provides a model for musicians who want to push the genre's limits without sacrificing its essential characteristics. His dedication to sincerity and narrative will serve as an inspiration to other songwriters, preserving the core of country music.

Toby Keith's accomplishments and industry recognition are evidence of his influence, skill, and commitment. Keith has had a profound impact on the country music scene, as seen by his several accolades, chart-topping tunes, and lasting influence. His dedication to family, charity, and activism, in addition to his musical accomplishments, define his legacy.

Keith will surely continue to have a major impact in the country music industry as he develops as an artist and a person. His legacy will go on for many years because of his capacity to establish a personal connection with audiences and his commitment to sincerity and service. In the end, Toby Keith is more than just a well-known figure in country music; he is a cultural icon whose influence reaches beyond the genre and leaves a deep mark on the emotions and thoughts of followers everywhere.

# Chapter 6: Ongoing Contributions and Upcoming Projects

Toby Keith's career has been distinguished by an unwavering desire for innovation and a dedication to his art, which have allowed him to hold a prominent position in the country music industry for many years. Even with his great success, Keith is still a developing artist who interacts with his fans, pursues new musical directions, and gives back to the community. This chapter explores Keith's latest endeavors and tours, the musical trajectories he is taking, and his outlook for the future.

## 6.1 Current Initiatives and Visits

Toby Keith has continued to be involved in the music industry by putting out new songs on a regular basis and interacting with fans live and on tour. The fact he keeps experimenting with different subjects and genres in his music without sacrificing the distinctive sound that has made him a household name is a testament to his dedication to his art.

Keith has put out a number of new songs in recent years, demonstrating his versatility in keeping with his original sound despite shifting musical trends. His sense of patriotism is evident in songs like "Happy Birthday America," which has always been a major part of his identity as a musician. In keeping with Keith's long-standing dedication to his nation and its people, this

2021 release is a celebration of American ideals and culture. The song, which appeals to listeners with its narrative aspects and traditional country feel, is a reflection of him going back to his origins.

Apart from being single, Keith has also worked on a number of group ventures. His flexibility and openness to new inspirations are shown by his ability to collaborate with various artists. Through partnerships with modern-day country musicians and songwriters, he has been able to experiment with many musical genres while keeping his distinctive narrative style. In the ever-changing world of country music, where fusing many genres and sounds has grown in popularity, this versatility is essential.

Keith's devotion to his fans and his art has also been shown by his recent travels. Large crowds still show up for his gigs, demonstrating his ongoing appeal in the business. Launched in 2022, the "Country Comes to Town" tour which combines his older songs with fresh material has gotten very positive reviews. By fusing memories with new material, Keith gives fans a captivating experience that strengthens the close bond he has developed with them over time.

In addition, Keith has prioritized helping out other musicians while on tour. He often has up-and-coming artists open for him, giving them a platform and a chance to perform for larger crowds. His dedication to coaching the next generation of musicians is a reflection of his conviction that developing potential within the country music industry is crucial.

Keith has increased his popularity and impact even further by taking part in a number of music festivals and events in addition to his concert tours. In addition to showcasing his musical prowess, his ability to interact with fans during live concerts further solidifies his standing as a highly regarded figure in the country music industry. Keith keeps establishing his reputation in the business by giving strong performances and establishing a connection with the crowd.

## 6.2 Novel Approaches to Music

Toby Keith has shown a willingness to experiment with many musical styles, even though he has established a successful career on the basis of conventional country music. This flexibility is essential in a field that is always changing, and Keith's openness to trying out new genres has allowed his music to remain current and interesting.

Keith has been experimenting with modern country-pop in recent years, fusing appealing tunes with cutting-edge production methods. This change is indicative of a larger trend in the genre, as musicians are progressively fusing mainstream elements to appeal to a wider range of listeners. Keith has been able to experiment with new sounds while keeping the essential parts of country music that his fans like because of his collaborations with pop and rock producers.

His partnership with modern country musicians is a noteworthy illustration of this inquiry, since it has enabled him to blend many genres and connect with a younger demographic. Keith's adaptability and readiness to adjust to shifting musical trends have been shown via his collaborations with musicians such as Miranda Lambert and Blake Shelton. Through this partnership, he has been able to reach a wider audience and broaden his musical repertoire, which will help to keep his music relevant in the modern world.

In order to interact with followers and release new songs, Keith has also embraced social media and digital channels. Keith has adjusted to the ways that social media and streaming services have transformed the way that musicians market their work. He has been able to communicate with fans via social media sites like Facebook and

Instagram, giving them access to exclusive material, behind-the-scenes looks at upcoming songs, and intimate details about his life and work. In a time when followers demand openness and sincerity, this direct interaction helps him build a feeling of community and connection with his audience.

Keith has also looked at topics that are relevant to modern problems. His willingness to use music to discuss social issues and current events shows how relevant he is as an artist. For example, he recorded songs during the COVID-19 epidemic that depicted the challenges and victories of people dealing with the situation. This strategy not only demonstrates his versatility but also his dedication to leveraging his position to solve significant social concerns.

Keith's commitment to developing as an artist is shown by his pursuit of new musical avenues. He stays true to his origins while welcoming change, which keeps people interested and advances the genre of country music.

## 6.3 Future Prospects

Toby Keith's outlook for the future includes a dedication to sustained innovation, involvement in the community, and assistance for up-and-coming musicians. Keith explores new avenues and stays true to his principles as he makes his way through the ever-changing music business.

To keep making music that connects with his listeners is one of Keith's main objectives going forward. Recognizing the value of narrative and genuineness in country music, he strives to write songs that capture the feelings and experiences of his listeners. Keith is committed to writing songs that have a profound emotional impact on listeners, whether via personal tales or larger issues.

In addition, Keith's dedication to community service and charity continues to be a pillar of his future plans. In order to find innovative methods of helping children with cancer and their families, he intends to increase the Toby Keith Foundation's activities. He wants to have a long-lasting effect on the lives of individuals in need and encourage other people in the business to become involved in charitable endeavors by sticking up for these causes.

Keith also has a strong desire to coach the next generation of country music performers. He thinks it's critical to help up-and-coming talent by giving them the tools and chances they need to be successful. He intends to keep working with up-and-coming musicians in the studio and showcasing them in his shows as part of this commitment. Keith wants to encourage young artists and assist them in overcoming the obstacles in the music business by sharing his experiences and wisdom.

Keith also sees a strong focus on creative innovation and cooperation in his future plans. He is excited to experiment with different sounds and genres as he understands that the music business is always changing. He wants to make new, creative music that stays loyal to his origins while reflecting the evolving country music scene by working with a variety of producers and musicians.

Apart from his musical endeavors, Keith is committed to using his influence to promote critical social causes. He intends to keep bringing up current issues in his songs and public remarks, highlighting the value of empathy, comprehension, and support from the community. By addressing pertinent subjects, he seeks to promote discussion and spur constructive social change.

Lastly, Keith sees a world in which the lively and varied genre of country music survives and grows. He thinks that despite differences, music has the ability to unite people and create relationships. Keith is steadfast in his commitment to advancing diversity and honoring the diverse range of voices within the country music industry as he pursues his career.

Toby Keith's enduring commitment to music, charity, and community is shown by his ongoing contributions and upcoming undertakings. Keith embodies the essence of a real artist dedicated to development and authenticity as he takes on new endeavors, pursues creative paths, and stays involved with his audience.

His most recent endeavors and live performances demonstrate his capacity to engage audiences while producing new, timely music. He keeps up with the shifting demands of the business by working with a varied range of musicians and trying out new techniques. Keith wants to make sure that his legacy lives on beyond his musical achievements, which is why he values social activism, mentoring, and storytelling in his future plans.

Looking forward, Toby Keith continues to have a major influence in the country music industry, motivating fans and musicians alike in the generations to come. His long influence on the genre and society at large is shown by his dedication to innovation, community, and compassion. Keith is well-positioned to make significant contributions to the music industry and beyond for many years to come because of his unwavering devotion to his profession and moral principles.

Printed in the USA
CPSIA information can be obtained
at www.ICGtesting.com
LVHW020301111224
798851LV00009B/562